Death, Where is Your Sting?

A Catholic Approach to Death

by Regis J. Flaherty

Steubenville, Ohio
A Division of Catholics United for the Faith
www.emmausroad.org

Emmaus Road Publishing
827 North Fourth Street • Steubenville, Ohio 43952

Printed in the United States of America
14 13 12 11   1 2 3 4 5

Library of Congress Control Number: 2011934214
ISBN: 978-1-937155-30-8

Cover design and layout by Julie Davis, General Glyphics, Inc., Dallas, Texas (www.glyphnet.com)

Nihil Obstat: Censor Librorum, Diocese of Pittsburgh
Imprimatur: Most Rev. David A. Zubik, DD, Bishop of Pittsburgh
July 8, 2010

The *nihil obstat* and *imprimatur* are official declarations that a work is considered to be free from doctrinal or moral error. It is not implied that those who have granted the same agree with the content, opinions, or statements expressed.

Death,
Where is Your Sting?

To all those with whom I have worked
in the apostolate of Catholic burial.
They regularly administer two of the Works of Mercy:
To bury the dead
To pray for the living and the dead

Contents

Introduction

My brothers and I slept on the third floor of my parents' home in Western Pennsylvania. There was no insulation in the walls, no heat, and no air conditioning. So it was sweltering in the summer and freezing in the winter. It was a great day when my parents purchased a window air conditioner for us. However, there was one problem. The air conditioner would not fit in the window. To enjoy a bit of cool air we had to first remove the exterior window frame. We didn't have a ladder that would reach the window, which was three and a half stories up. The answer? While sitting on the window ledge, I would lean out and remove the frame while my brothers held my legs inside. We would then install the air conditioner. The reverse process would occur every fall when we removed the unit.

One fall, when I was about nineteen or twenty years old, I decided I could remove the unit and replace the frame without help (I never was too bright!). First, I pulled a heavy cedar chest over to the window. After removing the air conditioner, I placed my feet under the trunk, took the frame, sat on the ledge, and leaned out the window. Holding the frame with one hand, I intended to use the other hand to turn the screws to complete the task. I was fully confident that my feet under the chest would allow me to defy gravity. I was wrong. The dresser suddenly moved, and gravity began to do what it does best. I was falling.

Flinging aside the frame and the screwdriver, I was able to grasp the window ledge with one hand just as my left knee struck the inside frame. From this precarious position I was able to pull myself back inside the room. Yes, I have thanked my guardian angel and look forward to thanking him face-to-face some day.

What I most remember about the incident is what flashed through my mind in those few seconds. First, it occurred to me that I was going to fall three and a half stories to my death. Next, I experienced fear. Then, I felt intense anger, certainly at my foolishness, but also at death itself. How could death claim me at this young age?

Since then I've learned that, when people recognize their mortality or that of those they love, they often experience fear and anger—the same emotions I felt in those seconds of falling. People fear their own death and often, as part of grieving, experience anger at the death of someone they love.

Powerful Feelings

Death evokes strong emotions in us, whether because of our own approaching death (many experience fear) or the death of a loved one (anger at the "loss"). Themes surrounding death—the pain, the confusion, the unfairness, the horror, the questioning—fill literature. Perhaps only the theme of love is more often a topic. Death comes to the wealthy and the poor, to the atheist and the religious, to the intelligent and the mentally challenged, and to the socially popular and the outcast.

Death is the ultimate equalizer. We all will die. What varies is how individuals handle death. For some it evokes horror and despair. For others it is quiet acceptance. Still others embrace death with a surety of hope and faith. All religions have a philosophy and a belief system to help adherents of that faith cope with this final reality.

What meaning can we find in death? This is not primarily a philosophical question, and it is not food for frivolous discussions. No, the question grabs us at a gut level. Its answer can be the difference between hope and despair. The Catholic Church promises an answer in the deposit of truth that it has cherished and protected since our Savior ascended into heaven with the promise of a return.*

Let us explore what Catholic faith tells us.

* This booklet doesn't have enough pages to pursue the thread of the argument that the Catholic Church possesses the fullness of truth. For further reading on that subject I suggest *Mere Catholicism* by Father Ian Ker, published by Emmaus Road Publishing. Also, we won't be able to fully explore the richness of the Church's teachings and understanding of how eternal realities are to form our approach to living. For a more expansive treatment of that theme I suggest my book *Last Things First,* published by Our Sunday Visitor, and available from Emmaus Road Publishing (www.emmausroad.org).

Death: Friend or Foe?

From a Catholic perspective, is death a friend or a foe? The answer? It is both.

Our primordial parents in the Garden of Eden would not have faced death, at least not the type of death that we experience, with its pain, aloneness, and alienation from the living. God told Adam and Eve that they were permitted—in fact, welcome—to eat from all of the fruit in the garden. The lone exception was the fruit of the tree of the knowledge of good and evil. That fruit was poison indeed. It was a deadly meal. God told our first parents that "in the day that you eat of it you shall die" (Gen. 2:17).

We know the story. Adam and Eve used their free will to disobey rather than love and honor God. They bought into the lie of the devil and disobeyed

God. Judgment fell swiftly upon them, and God banished them from Eden, telling them, "In the sweat of your face you shall eat bread till you return to the ground, for out of it you were taken; you are dust, and *to dust you shall return*" (Gen. 3:19, emphasis added). This has been the inheritance of man ever since. Even the most fortunate of men and women will experience suffering and will die.

Yet even as Adam and Eve were leaving the bliss of God's garden and entering the struggles that they had chosen by their sin, God showed mercy. He provided them with coverings to help them in the new and hostile environment (Gen. 3:21). He offered hope and made a promise of future redemption* (Gen. 3:15).

Man was not capable of righting the wrong. In this case he could not pull himself up by his bootstraps. God was needed and God provided in the fullness of time. Jesus, fully God and truly man, was born of a virgin. The Son of man came to crush the head of the same serpent who was the tempter in the garden. Christ embraced a death that would shatter death's power. In the garden on the Mount of Gethsemane He used His free will to reverse

* For more on the protoevangelium ("first Gospel"), see CCC 410.

what had occurred in another garden, the Garden of Eden. Jesus chose to obey and love His Father and to love all His brothers and sisters—us.

Christ truly died on the Cross. It was not faked, and it was not a trick or sleight of hand. His death was the real thing, involving pain, aloneness, and removal from the living. Yet when He bowed His thorn-crowned head and uttered the earth-shaking words, "It is finished" (Jn. 19:30), it was not His life that was finished but rather the reign of death. Christ was laid in a tomb but only to burst forth, pushing aside the stone that separated the dead from the living, a stone that symbolized the death sentence of all humanity. By His Resurrection not only was the tomb's stone thrust aside, but the very gates of heaven were opened.

Now we, with everyone who has died before Christ, with everyone who has died since Christ, and with everyone who will die, can shout in the face of death: "O death, where is thy victory? O death, where is thy sting?" (1 Cor. 15:55).

Where Is the Victory?

If Christ conquered death and has shared His Resurrection with us, why do we still experience death with the pain, aloneness, confusion, and separation that accompanies it? Were then the sin of Adam and the power of the tempter so strong in its evil that even God could not overcome it?

No! Christ *has* overcome death. "The Christian meaning of death is revealed in the light of the *Paschal mystery* of the death and resurrection of Christ in whom resides our only hope. The Christian who dies in Christ Jesus is 'away from the body and at home with the Lord'*" (CCC 1681). Yet it does take the eyes of faith to see the victory clearly. Scripture tells us that in this life our sight is blurred. "At present we see indistinctly, as in a mirror, but *then* face to face. At present I know partially; *then* I shall know fully, as I am fully known" (1 Cor. 13:12, NAB, emphasis added).

The reality of the defeat of death and the promise of resurrection are given to us now sacramentally. That does not make the truth less real. In fact, the reality is rock solid because it is based upon Christ

* 2 Cor. 5:8.

and His salvific work. Sacraments "are efficacious signs of grace, instituted by Christ and entrusted to the Church, by which divine life is dispensed to us. … They bear fruit in those who receive them with the required dispositions" (CCC 1131).

Any comparison of a heavenly reality with an earthly example will limp. However, comparisons can help our minds wrap around the divine truth.

If I receive a wound, the doctor will stitch my skin, closing the wound. Thereby the problem of an open wound is resolved, but I'll continue to see the sutures, at least for a time, and the scar will only gradually fade. Another example? If a wealthy man gives a pauper a checkbook, he is no longer poor. Yet until he cashes a check and realizes the fruit of the gift he will still look like and live as a pauper.

Now let's move to the spiritual reality and apply our comparisons. The hope of resurrection is realized in the Sacrament of Baptism. It is a hope that is sure (see Tit. 3:4–8). That sacrament deals with the wound we have inherited from our first parents, called *original sin*. Yet we will still see the effects while we walk this earth. Even after Baptism, concupiscence still troubles us. The *Catechism of the Catholic Church* teaches that, "certain temporal consequences of sin remain in the baptized, such as suffering, illness, death, and such frailties inherent in life as weaknesses of character, and so on, as well as an inclination to sin that Tradition calls *concupiscence*, or metaphorically, 'the tinder for sin'" (CCC 1264). We still live with a "scar."

God gives us what we need both to respond to Him and to persevere, such that we will enter into a heavenly relationship with the Triune God when our physical life is ended. Through Baptism we become God's children. Jesus, therefore, is our Brother. He is the Firstborn (Rev. 1:5) who has gone into the heavens to prepare a place for the rest of the family (Jn. 14:2). The door is open from the inside. We, the living, still stand outside, but we are gifted with all the help we will need to make the short trip through this life and enter into eternal bliss. Christ, who has shattered sin and death, gives us help to endure in this life, and to triumph in the next. The Church names that help *grace.* It "is *favor,* the *free and undeserved help* that God gives us to respond to his call to become children of God, adoptive sons, partakers of the divine nature and of *eternal life* [emphasis added]" (CCC 1996). It's as good as money in the bank. Similar to our example of the bank and the pauper above, we need only to draw down from the deposit He has given. The freedom of the children of God countermands the servitude of sin. The recipient truly is incorporated into Christ. He or she does receive grace and the theological virtues of faith, hope, and charity. By nurturing these gifts, each of the baptized will see the full flower of his or her hopes.

In Christ the victory is assured. The wound has been sutured, even though the scar is still evident. The money is in the bank, but we have yet to realize the fullness of the gift. Scripture tells us that Jesus is "the first-born of the dead" (Rev. 1:5). And the Church teaches: "Through Baptism the Christian is sacramentally assimilated to Jesus, who in his own baptism anticipates his death and resurrection. The Christian must enter into this mystery of humble self-abasement and repentance, ... so as to become the Father's beloved son in the Son and 'walk in newness of life'*" (CCC 537).

* Rom. 6:4.

Not Foe but Friend?

Okay, death is no longer our foe, but how is it *really* our friend?

Certainly we were all born to die. That's a true statement, but it only points to a partial reality. For fuller understanding we need to peer into what lies beyond our physical death. Yes, death is the end of physical life as we know it now, but death is also a *birth* into a greater life. Our physical death is actually a second birth. Let me explain.

From the time that we were conceived, we lived in the confined space of our mother's womb. After about nine months we were born into a vast new world—our first birth. Yet our life did not begin at physical birth; we had been an individual since conception. Actually, it would be accurate to say that our birth into the physical environment with which we are daily in contact—this world of blue skies, sunshine, solid food—was a death to the life we knew in the womb. At that first birth, life was not ended but changed.

One day we will leave this physical world where, right now, we feel so much at home. Our friends and relatives will proclaim our death, but they could equally say that we have been born into eternal life. We will leave this confining existence on planet Earth for the much more expansive existence of life that is forever. Just as the baby in the womb couldn't imagine what life would be like outside his mother's uterus, so we struggle to imagine what life will be like on the other side of the grave.

We can say that this birth at death—the second birth—will also be our final birth. We were made to enjoy life with God. It was the plan of God for Adam and Eve. It is God's plan for you and me. It is the plan for the last man or woman who will perish at the end of the physical world.

What can we expect in eternal life? The Church tells us that in heaven we will experience "the beatific vision, in which God opens himself in an inexhaustible way to the elect, [which] will be the ever-flowing well-spring of happiness, peace, and mutual communion" (CCC 1045). Not very specific, but perhaps it is the most we can say from the view here in our limited physical reality we have here. Nonetheless, we know that words like grand, awesome, spectacular, and any other superlatives in the English vocabulary fall short in describing the destiny for which we hope: falling not into oblivion but into the arms of God.

The anniversary of the death of a family member or friend is as much a date to celebrate as that day when some doctor spanked us so that we would begin breathing the air in this world. In fact, the feast day of most saints in the Church's liturgical calendar is the day that they died—left this life with all its struggles and limits—and began their heavenly existence.

The saints often would look to their death with joy and expectation because they longed for closer union with God. Saint Paul said, "We would rather leave the body and go home to the Lord" (2 Cor. 5:8, NAB). Paul saw death as a friend that would carry him to the Lord.

Saint Francis of Assisi saw death as even more than a friend. He praised God for "sister death." When Francis was approaching his own death he added the following stanza to his famous prayer, "The Canticle of the Sun":

Praised be You, my Lord through Sister Death,
from whom no one living can escape.
Woe to those who die in mortal sin!
Blessed are they She finds doing Your Will.
No second death can do them harm.

Every person whom death finds doing God's will is "blessed."

We must pause here because there is a caveat that we must consider. Let us explore the fuller truth.

Final Destinations

Death is a birth into eternal life, but not everyone will have the same destination. There will be a day of reckoning, the particular judgment, for each and every person at the time of death. Those who are "found in Christ" will enjoy a heavenly existence. Yet there is another possibility, to which Saint Francis alludes in his poem-prayer: "Woe to those who die in mortal sin!" The *Catechism* teaches, "Each man receives his eternal retribution in his immortal soul at the very moment of his death, in a particular judgment that refers his life to Christ: either entrance into the blessedness of heaven—through a purification or immediately,—or immediate and everlasting damnation*" (CCC 1022).

---

* Cf. Council of Lyons II (1274), Council of Florence (1439), Council of Trent (1563); cf. Benedict XII, *Benedictus Deus* (1336); cf. John XXII, *Ne super his* (1334).

Everlasting damnation will be the destination of some on their day of judgment. How many will experience that fate? We don't know, but we do know that hell exists. Certainly the fallen angels are there, and Scripture tells us those who fail the test of love are also destined for hell. They "will go away into eternal punishment" (Mt. 25:46). Certainly that thought should give us pause!

God's grace is given to us; His door is open; His arm is extended. What is needful is our response. Heaven is denied those who die in the state of mortal sin. We cannot judge the fate of individuals—mercifully, that is reserved to God—but the Church teaches clearly:

> *To choose deliberately—that is, both knowing it and willing it—something gravely contrary to the divine law and to the ultimate end of man is to commit a mortal sin. This destroys in us the charity without which eternal beatitude is impossible. Unrepented, it brings eternal death. (CCC 1874)*

This "eternal death" is what Saint Francis calls "second death" in his Canticle of the Sun. The damned eternally are bereft of the relationship with God that He intended for them. Ultimately the options are simple. Heaven is to be with God. Hell is the total absence of God. Those who reject the Almighty freely choose all the horrors of hell.

This is a sobering thought; yet it should not lead us to debilitating fear. We must strive to fully live out the consequences of our baptism—a daily decision of our will—while knowing that ultimately we rely on the mercy of God.*

Purification after Death

You may have noticed that the quotation from the *Catechism* addressing entrance into the blessedness of heaven states that it may happen "through a purification or immediately" (CCC 1022). Some people when they die will be ready to go straight to heaven. As with those bound for hell, we have no indication of how many will take the direct route to glory. However, it is safe to say that many of us will need to undergo a further purification after death before we can stand before an all-holy God. This is because "every sin, even venial, entails an

* See chapter 10 in my book *Last Things First* for a fuller treatment of the demands of Baptism.

unhealthy attachment to creatures, which must be purified either here on earth, or after death in the state called Purgatory. This purification frees one from what is called the 'temporal punishment' of sin" (CCC 1472).

It is first of all important to note that purgatory is for those who have died in the state of grace. At death a person's fate is sealed. He is either bound for heaven or hell. Purgatory is not an option for the damned. However, it is a merciful provision for those who require further purification prior to heavenly life.

Purgatory is not a place but rather a process. It has been explained in various ways. At times it has been referred to as fire that burns away the dross of our lives until only the pure "gold" of sanctity remains. Others liken it to a process where we let go of all that we have held so dearly on earth so that we can receive the great gift of heaven with open and empty hands.

Whatever the imagery we use, the reality is the same. Purgatory is a process of purification that ends in full admittance into the heavenly relationship with God.

Love Reaches beyond the Grave

After the death of a loved one, people often struggle because of the separation they experience. In truth, the deceased is no longer physically present; yet the Church teaches that a vital connection remains between the living and the deceased who are in heaven or undergoing the purification of purgatory. All of the faithful are united in the Mystical Body of Christ. Those in heaven (the Church Triumphant), those in purgatory (the Church Suffering), and those of us still on earth (the Church Militant) are united in the one Body of Christ. Jesus is the head of the Body and it is His life-blood that flows through all of the members that are united to Him. Therefore, the three groups are united to each other. Consequently, we know that we can effectively ask the saints to pray for us in our struggles here on earth, just as we might ask for help from our neighbor who lives in the house across the street.

Also, since we remain connected to those in purgatory, we can impact their lives in an effective way.

To Pray for the Dead

While working for Catholic cemetery organizations I cannot tell you how often I saw someone standing at the grave of a spouse or other loved one, talking to the deceased. I've done it myself, and imagine many of you have also done so. There is something inside of us that rebels at the idea that death completely separates us from those we love. We have a godly desire to continue to help our beloved deceased. Here is a portion of what Cardinal Joseph Ratzinger (Pope Benedict XVI) has said on the topic:

> *Few things are as immediate, as human and as widespread—at all times and in all cultures—as prayer for one's own departed dear ones. … Praying for one's departed loved ones is a far too immediate urge to be suppressed; it*

> *is a most beautiful manifestation of solidarity, love and assistance, reaching beyond the barrier of death. The happiness or unhappiness of a person dear to me, who has now crossed to the other shore, depends in part on whether I remember or forget him; he does not stop needing my love.*[*]

We can help those in purgatory by praying for them and by offering sacrifices on their behalf. Also, the greatest prayer, the Mass, can be offered for the faithful departed. The *Catechism* teaches: "From the beginning the Church has honored the memory of the dead and offered prayers in suffrage for them, above all the Eucharistic sacrifice, so that, thus purified, they may attain the beatific vision of God.[†] The Church also commends almsgiving, indulgences, and works of penance undertaken on behalf of the dead" (CCC 1032).

---

* Joseph Cardinal Ratzinger, *The Ratzinger Report: An Exclusive Interview on the State of the Church, with Vittorio Messori* (San Francisco: Ignatius Press, 1985), 146–47.

† Cf. Council of Lyons II (1274).

A Road Map for the Journey

If you want to understand how we remain connected to the deceased, the *Catechism of the Catholic Church* is an invaluable tool, which I've quoted a number of times in the preceding sections of this booklet. The *Catechism* opens the Scripture and Tradition in an orderly and logical way. It's a tool for the left-brainers* among us. Yet the *Catechism* also points to another excellent source that helps us appreciate the truth of the Catholic faith. The liturgical ceremonies of the Church that surround death and burial speak to right side of the brain.

* The left side of the brain is associated with an analytical approach. The right side is associated with aesthetics and a holistic approach.

What the Liturgy Reveals

If you're going to take a trip to a place you've never before visited, it is very helpful to have a map. A good road map or a GPS device will show the best route for arriving at the desired destination. Information on road hazards, possible alternate routes, and places to stop for a rest make the travel easier. There is no doubt; a map can make all the difference between a successful trip and one fraught with confusion and frustration.

A Catholic funeral is a type of journey. The *Order of Christian Funerals* (hereafter OCF) gives us an opportunity to walk as a community of faith with the deceased and the surviving family and friends. In fact, the Catholic Church in the "General Introduction" to the OCF identifies the Christian funeral as the "last journey" for the body of the deceased. There are three major divisions of the OCF, each of which relates to a major stop along that journey.

You are probably familiar with parts of that final journey. You may have visited a funeral home, attended a funeral Mass, or witnessed a committal at a cemetery—the major stops on the road.

However, at some point in your life you will likely experience the death of someone who is very close to you: a spouse, a parent, a child. In these situations you will be the person primarily responsible for the funeral and burial. You won't merely be making the trip; you will be the "driver." The Catholic "map" gives not only direction but also consolation.

The Church has provided a great help in the prayers and liturgies for a Christian funeral. The OCF provides encouragement, support, a godly focus, and the perspective of a "hope [that] does not disappoint" (Rom. 5:5).

Accompanying the body of a departed love one on that final journey provides great benefits for the surviving family members. It gives them another opportunity to express their love and to honor the person who has died.

There are three "stages" or "stations" to the Catholic Funeral Rite (see OCF 42):

1. The Vigil for the Deceased, the time immediately after death until the Funeral Liturgy
2. The Funeral Liturgy, usually a Mass
3. The Rite of Committal, the conclusion of the Funeral Rite which normally occurs at the cemetery

The Vigil and Related Prayers

The first rite, or stage, which the Church offers is the prayers that follow after the death but before the Funeral Mass. These rites include prayers that can be said immediately after the death, when family first gathers in the presence of the body, when the body is transferred to the Church, and at the vigil for the deceased.

Prayers after Death

In the OCF, prayers are offered not only for the deceased but also for the family. The initial prayer encourages those gathered with the Scripture "Blessed are those who mourn, for they shall be comforted" (Mt. 5:4). From where does this comfort come? Because of His love, it is from "God himself who will always be with them" (Rev. 21:3, NAB).

Indeed, God can give peace to those who grieve. It is a peace that the world cannot give—one that is beyond understanding. In truth, God "can wipe away every tear from their eyes" (Rev. 21:4).

There are three Scripture readings suggested for these initial prayers after a death (in fact all of the prayers and rites from the OCF are scripturally based). One is from the eleventh chapter of the Gospel of John (vv. 17–44), where Jesus comforts Mary and Martha at the death of their brother Lazarus. Jesus tells the sisters that He is Lord over death and that in Him the faithful never really die. Instead, they are born into a new life. Jesus then shows the power behind His words as He brings Lazarus back to life. The promise is the same for those who gather after the death of someone close to them. Jesus does bring life, and in that the mourners can find comfort.

Gathering in the Presence of the Body

The timing of the rite of "Gathering in the Presence of the Body" can vary based on the needs of the family. It may occur before the body is prepared for the viewing or the burial, or after that preparation. It may also occur when the family first gathers at the funeral home for the wake.

These prayers start with the making of the Sign of the Cross. How fitting to begin with a prayer that harkens back to Baptism, the sacrament that brings us into the Family of God. This sacrament gives the one who receives it an "indelible mark" that identifies the baptized person as a son or daughter of God.

In death it is that relationship that is the source of our hope. The Father is waiting to welcome His children. During this rite the minister also sprinkles the body of the deceased with holy water. This action too brings to mind the Sacrament of Baptism that cleansed us of sin. The Church recommends two psalms for reflection during this gathering at the body of the deceased. Psalm 130 is the prayer of one who calls from the "depths" asking God to hear his prayers. It is a prayer of trust in God "for with the Lord there is steadfast love, and with him is plenteous redemption" (v. 7). The perspective of Psalm 116 also consoles: indeed, "precious in the sight of the Lord is the death of his servants (v. 15)."

Transfer of the Body

The concept that physical death is part of a larger journey to our eternal home is emphasized in the prayers for the "Transfer of the Body to the Church or to the Place of Burial." Psalm 122 is most fitting for this rite. This psalm is one of the "Psalms of Ascent," which were prayed as pilgrims processed to the Temple in Jerusalem.

I rejoiced when they said to me:
"Let us go to the house of the Lord."
And now our feet are standing
within your gates, Jerusalem.
(Ps. 122:1–2, NAB)

In a Catholic funeral the deceased is on a journey to the heavenly Jerusalem, of which the earthly Temple was but a sign. There is sorrow in this journey, but those who grieve should not lose sight of the inherent joy for those who are in Christ. The concluding prayer for the "Transfer of the Body" acknowledges that the deceased has left this "earthly dwelling," but with the hope of entrance into the heavenly kingdom where we can join him or her in the future.

The Vigil for the Deceased

The "Vigil for the Deceased" is a time when the Christian community and the friends and family of the deceased pray and keep watch together. It is a time to support one another and reflect on the mercy of God and the strength that He gives us. The vigil consists of four parts: the introductory rites; the Liturgy of the Word, which can include a homily; prayers of intercession; and a concluding rite and blessing.

A priest or deacon will often lead the vigil, but a layperson, with slight modification of the rite, can also preside.* The Church community is also encouraged to join the family in the celebration.

The opening prayer first acknowledges that it is because of the death and Resurrection of Jesus that both the deceased and the living have access to the blessedness of heaven. The prayer then seeks the mercy of God upon the deceased, asking that he or she would be worthy of heaven. Two profound truths are presented in this prayer.

First, all is grace! We don't get to heaven because we were good, attended Mass regularly, kept the commandments better than our next-door neighbor, or gave more in the parish collection that fifty percent of the parishioners. All of these are important and are signs of a life given to Christ. However, on our own we cannot merit heaven. Heaven is a free gift. So those at the vigil commend the deceased to the mercy of God.

---

* For the rites in the OCF the pastor or associate pastor is viewed as the normal minister. However, with the exception of the Funeral Mass, a deacon or a layperson can preside when necessary with appropriate modifications to the rite.

The opening prayer also serves as a reminder to the living. We have free will. We can refuse or reject the salvation given by Christ. Mourning the death of someone we love brings our own mortality into focus. We must choose Christ so as to partake of the mercy and grace that He offers.

The readings in the Liturgy of the Word are on the theme of eternal life (for example, 1 Cor. 5:1, 6–10 and Lk. 12:35–40). The responsorial between the readings is taken from Psalm 27. It is a prayer of praise that both consoles and challenges those in attendance to focus on God's protection and mercy.

The Lord is my light and my salvation;
whom shall I fear?
The Lord is the stronghold of my life;
of whom shall I be afraid?

When evildoers assail me,
uttering slanders against me,
my adversaries and foes,
they shall stumble and fall.

Though a host encamp against me,
my heart shall not fear;
though war arise against me,
yet I will be confident.

One thing have I asked of the Lord,
that will I seek after;
that I may dwell in the house of the Lord
all the days of my life,
to behold the beauty of the Lord,
and to inquire in his temple.

For he will hide me in his shelter
in the day of trouble;
he will conceal me under the cover of his tent,
he will set me high upon a rock. …

I believe that I shall see the goodness of the Lord
in the land of the living!
Wait for the Lord;
be strong, and let your heart take courage;
yea, wait for the Lord! (Ps. 27:1–5, 13–14)

The intercessions, which follow the readings, ask the Lord for grace and comfort. The response of the congregation is "Lord, have mercy."

The concluding prayer summarizes the entire focus of the vigil. Jesus is the Redeemer, who willingly gave Himself over to death so that all of us could receive salvation and eternal life with His and our Father. The prayer then asks that the grieving be comforted and the deceased be received "into the arms of mercy." Jesus, who has opened the doors of heaven and offered forgiveness through His life, death, and Resurrection, is asked to bring the deceased to "a place of happiness, light, and peace" to dwell there forever.

Funeral Mass

The next major stop on the journey is the Funeral Mass. The Mass is the most fitting and powerful of prayers, and can be offered for the intention of the deceased person. It is also a sign of the unity of the living and the deceased, for in the Mass we enter into something that is eternal. The Mass, which we celebrate in our churches, is a re-presentation of the sacrifice of Calvary. The suffering, death, and Resurrection of Christ are the means of salvation—both for us and for the deceased. Indeed, "there is salvation in no one else, for there is no other name under heaven given among men by which we must be saved" (Acts 4:12).

Many sacramentals are used within the Funeral Liturgy to remind us of various aspects of the journey to eternal life.

A large candle is set at the head of the casket. That candle was first blessed and lit at the Easter Vigil as a symbol of the risen Christ who is the light of the world. At the beginning of the Easter Vigil Mass the Church had been in darkness as it awaited the risen Lord. The Easter candle had brought light to the darkness. In Christ, darkness is banished, and new life is seen in His light. That Paschal light, on display at the Funeral Mass, reminds everyone in attendance that our sorrow must always be tempered by the joy and hope we have in Christ.

The Easter candle is also another reminder of Baptism, for a similar Paschal candle was present at the individual's baptism. The family life of the Trinity, entered at Baptism, comes to a new level of intimacy in death.

During the "Final Commendation," which normally occurs subsequent to the prayer after Communion*, holy water is used.† It too is a sign of Baptism—the waters of salvation. The sprinkling is a form of farewell, while also an acknowledgement of the unity of all the baptized in the Body of Christ.

Incense is used in blessing the coffin. The rising aromatic smoke is a reminder that our prayers effectively reach our Lord Jesus, who is enthroned at the right hand of the Father. "The smoke of the incense along with the prayers of the holy ones went up before God" (Rev. 8:4, NAB). Our intercessions are joined with those of our Savior (see Rom. 8:34) in a united prayer to the Father.

As we smell the incense we are again reminded of Christ's victory over sin that He shares with the faithful. It gives us a moment also to praise Him—to echo the words of the author of the Book of Sirach:

---

* The Final Commendation may also occur at the place of committal.

† Holy water is also used at the vigil service and later at the committal.

Send forth fragrance like frankincense, and put forth blossoms like a lily.
Scatter the fragrance, and sing a hymn of praise;
bless the Lord for all his works;
ascribe majesty to his name
and give thanks to him with praise,
with songs on your lips, and with lyres;
and this you shall say in thanksgiving:
"All things are the works of the Lord, for they are very good,
and whatever he commands will be done in his time." (Sir. 39:14–16)

Committal

The final phase of a Catholic funeral is the "Rite of Committal." This usually takes place at the cemetery where the body of the faithful departed will be laid to rest. This is the final farewell to the body, but not to the relationship with the person if he or she is destined for purgatory or heaven.

At the beginning of the committal the minister invites all in attendance to assist the departed loved one with their prayers.

The service includes the committal prayer, which can take several forms. One prayer focuses particular attention on hope. We commend the deceased to Jesus, who is our sure and certain hope. This prayer follows Scripture, in which we are "strongly encouraged to hold fast to the hope that lies before us. This we have as an anchor of the soul, sure and firm, which reaches into the interior behind the veil, where Jesus has entered on our behalf as forerunner" (Heb. 6:18–19).

The intercessions follow, concluding with the Our Father and a final prayer for the deceased. The service ends with the minister offering a prayer for the surviving friends and family, that they would have strength, hope, and comfort in Christ.

Ongoing Prayer

The committal ends the Funeral Rite, but it is not the end of what we can do for the deceased and the family. We can continue to intercede for the living and the dead. We can also have the most powerful prayer, the Mass, offered for the departed.

Respect for the Dead

The *Catechism* reiterates a long-standing Jewish and Christian tradition of respect for the body of the deceased. Lack of proper respect for the physical remains of the dead is an offense against the Fifth Commandment: "You shall not kill."

"The bodies of the dead must be treated with respect and charity, in faith and hope of the Resurrection. The burial of the dead is a corporal work of mercy;* it honors the children of God, who are temples of the Holy Spirit" (CCC 2300). The body of the deceased represents an individual who has been loved by God. God loved that individual so much that Jesus gave His life for that person. The respectful and reverential handling of the funeral and burial is consistent with the value of each individual in God's eyes. People are not disposable.

* Cf. Tob. 1:16.

Whether rich or poor, they are precious in God's sight.

The Scriptures show that human life is a gift from God, and the people of the Old Covenant saw it as such. Even though, for most of Bible history, the Jews did not have a fully developed understanding of an afterlife, they nonetheless treated the body, in life and in death, with respect. Even the Temple priests, who tried Jesus and contributed to His crucifixion, used Judas' rejected blood money to buy a plot of land for the burial of poor foreigners (see Mt. 27:7).

There are a number of Scripture passages that emphasize the importance of respectful treatment of the dead. Those who fail to treat the body of the deceased appropriately are severely criticized. Meanwhile, those who reverently and faithfully bury the dead are praised. Tobit is identified as a just man because he buried the dead even when it put his life in danger:

> *In the days of Shalmaneser I performed many acts of charity to my brethren. I would give my bread to the hungry and my clothing to the naked; and if I saw any one of my people dead*

and thrown out behind the wall of Nineveh, I would bury him. And if Sennacherib the king put to death any who came fleeing from Judea, I buried them secretly. For in his anger he put many to death. When the bodies were sought by the king, they were not found. Then one of the men of Nineveh went and informed the king about me, that I was burying them; so I hid myself. When I learned that I was being searched for, to be put to death, I left home in fear. Then all my property was confiscated and nothing was left to me except my wife Anna and my son Tobias. (Tob. 1:16–20)

Appropriate grieving and a dignified burial are responsibilities that a pious man should not ignore. The author of Sirach writes: "My son, let your tears fall for the dead, and as one who is suffering grievously begin the lament. Lay out his body with the honor due him, and do not neglect his burial" (38:16).

The New Testament also shows the importance of the respectful handling of the body after death. After the crucifixion Jesus was wrapped in a shroud and placed in the tomb owned by Joseph of

Arimathea (see Lk. 23:50–53). Pious women who were followers of Jesus discovered that Christ had risen from the dead when they went to the tomb to anoint His body for burial (see Lk. 24:1–3). This anointing was a common Jewish practice that honored the deceased.

While dining at the house of Simon the Leper in Bethany, a woman came up to Jesus "with an alabaster jar of perfumed oil, costly genuine spikenard. She broke the alabaster jar and poured it on his head" (Mk. 14:4, NAB). When others at table complained of the expense and "waste" of the oil, Jesus pointed to the value of her action. "Jesus said, 'Let her alone. Why do you make trouble for her? She has done a good thing for me. … She has anticipated anointing my body for burial' " (Mk. 14:6–8).

A Worthy Vessel

Any vessels used for a religious purpose are to be treated with respect. The Church building is blessed and designated for a sacred purpose. Only appropriate activity is permitted within. If the Church is to be sold, there is a special ceremony that marks its transfer from sacred to secular use.

The chalice, paten, ciborium, and other liturgical items are treated with care and reserved only for use in the liturgy. Linens used at Mass are handled carefully and washed separately.

The human body in life held the soul—the breath of God—within it. In Baptism the Holy Spirit took up residence in that physical being. Every time that person received Holy Communion, Christ entered him or her in a tangible way. So, even in death, that body should be treated with the respect due any and every sacred object.

Cremation

Cremation continues to be a growing trend in many parts of the country. Some segments of the population are more open to cremation than other groups. Catholics have had a long tradition of opposition to cremation, so there is a great deal of confusion among Catholics about the appropriateness of cremation for the Catholic and about the regulations that govern such a choice. Since cremation raises so many questions, it is appropriate to review the topic in some depth.

History

The Jewish people of the Old Testament did not cremate their dead. The Bible reveals only one incidence of cremation. In 1 Samuel 31:12 it is recorded that the "body of Saul and the bodies of his sons … [were] burnt … [and] their bones buried." It is unclear why cremation was chosen in this one incident, but it does stand out as unusual, and certainly was not the norm.

Christians continued the tradition of burial, often risking their lives to recover the bodies of the martyrs and provide a respectful burial for these saints. The *Catholic Encyclopedia* states: "The pagans, to destroy faith in the resurrection of the body, often cast the corpses of martyred Christians into the flames, fondly believing thus to render impossible the resurrection of the body."* Catholic teachers refuted this belief, stating that cremation did not hinder God's power to raise the bodies of the deceased on the last day. Nevertheless, the

* William Devlin, "Cremation," in *The Catholic Encyclopedia*, vol. 4 (New York: Robert Appleton Company, 1908), available at www.newadvent.org/cathen/04481c.htm.

rhetoric of the pagans was probably an added reason for the Catholics to avoid cremation.

The prohibition against cremation continued through the Middle Ages. Pope Boniface VII in 1300 decreed that a body could not be cremated even for the purpose of transferring the remains to another location. Boniface wrote that "bodies are either to be conveyed whole to the spot chosen or buried at the place of death until, in the course of nature, the bones can be removed for burial elsewhere."* In fact, he stated that to disobey this directive was grounds for excommunication.

This continued to be the unopposed teaching of the Church well into the nineteenth century. In the late 1800s the Freemasons, a strongly anti-Catholic group, gained government permission in countries that were traditionally Catholic to cremate dead bodies in direct opposition to Church teaching. The Masons practiced cremation, at least in part, as a statement against the Catholic teaching of the resurrection of the body. Many cremation societies were formed in Europe to promote cremation.

The Church continued to prohibit cremation while still teaching that cremation was not a barrier

* Ibid.

to the resurrection of the body. Pope Leo XIII (1878–1903) approved the following rules concerning cremation:

- It was not permitted to join societies that had as a purpose the promotion of cremation.
- It was not permitted to direct that one's own body be cremated nor to cremate the body of another.
- If their bodies were cremated, but against their wills, the baptized could still receive Church funeral rites. This could take place in a church or home, but not at the place of cremation.
- If cremation was willed, "definitely and notoriously even until death," it was not permitted to give that person burial in a church.*

Modern Times

In our own time cremation has become much more accepted. Certainly few would advocate cremation as a statement of opposition to the resurrection of the body at the end of time. Nonetheless, the Church still favors traditional burial over cremation. Canon

* Available at www.catecheticsonline.com/SourcesofDogma19.php.

law shows this preference: "The Church earnestly recommends that the pious custom of burying the bodies of the deceased be observed; nevertheless, the Church does not prohibit cremation unless it was chosen for reasons contrary to Christian doctrine" (can. 1176§3). Traditional burial makes a connection between the physical body being buried and the glorified body that will dwell for eternity in the kingdom of God. The prayers of the Funeral Rite refer specifically to the "body." Also, traditional burial arguably emphasizes respect for the body in a way that cremation does not.

The moral theologian Germain Grisez gives an appropriate understanding of the Church's present approach:

> *Longstanding Catholic practice favors burying or entombing the corpses of the faithful departed, since doing so provides a fitting sign of the hope that those now resting in death will soon rise to everlasting life. Nevertheless, cremation has been permitted in the past when necessary for a grave reason, such as control of a contagious disease. Today, while the Church's law still encourages burial or entombment, it*

no longer forbids cremation, provided it is not chosen to express disbelief in the resurrection of the dead or for some other reason at odds with the faith. Therefore, a Catholic family may choose cremation if there is any other motive for preferring it.[*]

It is respect for the body that should be maintained no matter what the family chooses—full body burial or cremation. For this reason those who choose cremation are most strongly encourage to inter or entomb the cremated remains. The introduction to the 1997 appendix to the *Order of Christian Funerals* states:

The cremated remains of a body should be treated with the same respect given to the human body from which they come. This includes the use of a worthy vessel to contain the ashes, the manner in which they are carried, the care and attention to appropriate placement and transport, and the final disposition. The cremated remains should be buried in a grave or entombed in a mausoleum or columbarium.

---

* Germain Grisez, *The Way of the Lord, Volume Two: Living a Christian Life* (Quincy, IL: Franciscan Press, 1993), 719

The practice of scattering cremated remains ... or keeping cremated remains in the home of a relative or friend of the deceased are not the reverent disposition that the Church requires. Whenever possible, appropriate means for recording with dignity the memory of the deceased should be adopted, such as a plaque or stone which records the name of the deceased. (no. 417)

The OCF *on Cremation*

The *Order of Christian Funerals* for the United States, which was canonically approved in 1989, assumed that the Funeral Mass would be conducted with the full body present. The 1989 edition of the OCF made no provision for a Funeral Mass with the cremated remains rather than the full body. However, a substantial number of Catholic families who chose cremation had the body cremated prior to making arrangements for the Funeral Mass. This created a pastoral problem. The parish had to deny the Funeral Mass when the family brought cremated remains rather than the full body.

Responding to "numerous requests and concerns," in August 1996 the bishops of the United States requested an indult "to allow the presence of the cremated remains of a body at the Funeral Liturgy in dioceses of the United States." Indults "are general faculties ... granted by the Holy See to bishops and others, of doing something not permitted by the common law." An indult grants an exception to the norm in response to "peculiar local conditions." The Congregation for Divine Worship in March 1997 granted this request. The Vatican approved texts and rituals for use when the cremated remains are present at the Funeral Liturgy in July of the same year.

Even though cremated remains are now permitted at the Funeral Liturgy, the appendix to the OCF concerning cremation lists several important caveats:

- "Although cremation is ... permitted by the Church, it does not enjoy the same value as burial of a body" (no. 413).
- The cremated remains at the Funeral Liturgy are permitted in "extraordinary circumstances" (no. 413).

- It is still "recommended" that cremation "take place after the Funeral Liturgy" (no. 417).
- Each diocesan bishop has jurisdiction in his diocese to permit or deny the right to conduct the Funeral Mass (no. 427) in the presence of the cremated remains.
- The value of burial, especially in a Catholic cemetery, is emphasized (no. 417).

Paying for a Funeral

Respect for the body of the deceased does not mean that the most expensive casket or funeral is necessary or even desirable. Balance and prudence, not ostentation, are important. It is the full use of the OCF that is to be encouraged, not exquisite flower displays or stretch limousines. The moral theologian Germain Grisez emphasizes the benefit of a Catholic funeral and the "value of bringing family and friends together." He does, however, have a caution.

> *In many respects current funeral practices are neither reasonable nor Christian. In affluent societies, even families of modest means often succumb to the sales techniques of the funeral*

industry, unreasonable social expectations, and confused emotions, for example, a feeling of guilt unless they provide a lavish funeral.

Christian families should not feel compelled to conform to prevailing secular standards.[*]

---

* Grisez, *Living a Christian Life*, 719

New Heavens and a New Earth

In our contemplation of death, there is a manifestation of the kingdom of God that we still await. Scripture tells us: "According to his promise we wait for new heavens and a new earth" (2 Pet. 3:13).

In the creed at every Sunday Mass, Catholics proclaim: "I look forward to the resurrection of the dead, and the life of the world to come."

The resurrection of the body is a topic that focuses on the end times. The *Catechism of the Catholic Church* tells us that "at the end of the world*" God "will definitively grant incorruptible life to our bodies by reuniting them with our souls, through the power of Jesus' Resurrection" (CCC 1001 and 997).

However, to understand what will happen at the end of time, we need to reexamine the beginning of time. What was God's intent and plan when

* Jn. 6:39–40, 44, 54; 11:24; *Lumen Gentium* 48§3.

he created mankind? Adam and Eve were created "to share … in divine life" (CCC 375). Our first parents experienced an "inner harmony" between body and soul: "As long as he remained in the divine intimacy, man would not have to suffer or die" (CCC 376).

Man "*preferred* himself to God" (CCC 398). He lost his "inner harmony" and became subject to "bondage to decay*" (CCC 376, 400). Man would suffer in his work and life. Death made its entrance into human history.

The good news is that God did not abandon us. Jesus came and gave His life so that we can be reunited to God, and so that the original intent of creation could be restored.

Wait a minute! Jesus has come and we do experience the effects of His redemption. However, we still experience struggle and suffering. We often don't experience inner harmony. We get old. Our hair thins. Then we die and our bodies are subject to decay. At a quick glance we may be tempted to say that God's original order has not been restored. Our sin seems to have been more powerful and effective than Christ's suffering, death, and Resurrection.

---

* Rom. 8:21.

Nevertheless, Christ's Paschal mystery "liberates us from sin … and opens for us the way to a new life" (CCC 654). The fullness of Christ's work will only be seen at the end of time, when there will be a "new heavens and a new earth" (see Rev. 21:1). The epistle to the Hebrews tells us that we have only tasted "the powers of the age to come" (6:5). Our souls will be reunited with our glorified bodies. We will dwell with God in His kingdom. The beauty and glory of that kingdom will exceed even the Garden of Eden! Then we will be fully united with all of our brothers and sisters in the Family of God, including members of our own family.

Preparing for Death

When a family member is gripped by a terminal illness, those who love that person struggle with what to tell him or her. Sometimes, because of a misguided desire not to upset the sick person, a code of silence surrounds the individual. However, we all need to be prepared for death both physically and, more importantly, spiritually. It does no service to the dying to deny them the opportunity to prepare.

In a 2008 address at a convention of medical professionals, Bishop Elio Sgreccia, the president of the Pontifical Academy for Life, stated that it is "essential to be able to confront death when it arrives, because one has to make peace with death during life."* He pointed out that it is a disservice to hide pending death from the sick person. It is certainly never appropriate to lie. Instead, he

* Mirko Testa, "Bishop Sgreccia: Dying Have Right to Know" (January 16, 2008), available at www.zenit.org/article-21513?l=english.

encourages physicians and others to speak truth with charity.

The truth needs to be given to the dying within a faith context. Bishop Sgreccia said that the patient should be told "of the life that does not die and the revelation of Christ dead and risen, present and working in each man who suffers."

The physical suffering of the dying is passing; eternal life lies before them. To be deprived of the opportunity to use that time for spiritual preparation can be tragic.

On a number of occasions I've been asked to speak with the dying. I've told people that they are dying, and I've addressed spiritual concerns with them. I readily admit that these conversations are not easy and must be approached with charity and an understanding of the individual's circumstances, but also with determination. I recall one person who, despite a number of conversations, refused to accept that he was dying. At first he was happy for my visits, but eventually told me to leave because he didn't want to hear what needed to be said. I was told that with his last breaths he continued to deny that he was going to die.

However, I can also testify that this has been the exception. Most often people know that their condition is serious. They want to talk about their situation. Yet a standoff often results: the family is afraid to broach the subject of death to "spare the dying person," and the sick person doesn't want to bring up the subject because they see it makes their loved ones uncomfortable. This benefits neither the living nor the dying. True love often demands that we encourage the dying to prepare spiritually and to get right with God and the Church.

Anointing of the Sick

Three sacraments are especially important for a person in danger of dying. They are Reconciliation, Eucharist, and the Anointing of the Sick. The person who knows that death is near receives a real benefit from these sacraments. It gives him a time to "get right" with God and to prepare for meeting Him.

As some people are reluctant to talk about death, others, because of a desire not to disturb or frighten the dying person, are reluctant to call a priest for the anointing and reception of the other sacraments. This is a real disservice to the sick person. If the person is to die, it is best to face death with all the blessings and graces that are available through the Church. Also, at times the sacraments, especially the Anointing of the Sick, can bring physical healing or a lessening of pain.

When a priest comes to anoint a person, it is also an opportunity for the individual to receive two other sacraments: Reconciliation (Confession) and Eucharist. The Eucharist given to someone in danger of death is called *Viaticum*—food for the journey! You can do no greater service for someone in danger of death than to facilitate his or her reception of the sacraments.

One Other Thing to Remember

Death is inevitable. It is part of the human condition. The Church for two thousand years has encouraged an important perspective toward death: We should always be prepared to die. No one knows the day or the time that he or she will die. So we should always strive to avoid sin and live as children of God in the relationship that was established for each of us at our baptism. Saint Augustine wrote: "Live in such a way that when you die, you don't die." That should always be our goal—eternal life with our heavenly Father.

Conclusion

Death does evoke fear and anger. It is a part of the human condition that causes us pain. The Catholic faith brings light for the dark times that surround the "loss" of a loved one. Faith does not remove all sorrow and does not eliminate grief. However, it does bring perspective, hope, and opportunities to continue to love those who have died. Faith also points to an ultimate reality. If we persevere as Christians, in the fullness of time we will be united with all those who have loved God. For that we can be thankful.

The Faith Basics Series

- Death, Where Is Your Sting? A Catholic Approach to Death
- Come to the Celebration: The Church's Liturgical Year
- Prayer: A Catholic Perspective
- Sacramentals and Signs: Objects, Actions, and Words as Avenues for Grace
- Sacraments: The Seven Spiritual Wonders of the World
- Discovering the "Awe" of the Mass